North American
Animals

MOOSE

by Annie Hemstock

Consulting Editor: Gail Saunders-Smith, PhD

CAPSTONE PRESS
a capstone imprint

Pebble Plus is published by Capstone Press,
1710 Roe Crest Drive, North Mankato, Minnesota 56003.
www.capstonepub.com

Books published by Capstone Press are manufactured with paper
containing at least 10 percent post-consumer waste.

Library of Congress Cataloging-in-Publication Data
Hemstock, Annie.
  Moose / by Annie Hemstock.
      p. cm.—(Pebble plus. North American animals)
  Includes bibliographical references and index.
  Summary: "Simple text and full-color photographs provide a brief introduction to moose"—Provided by publisher.
  ISBN 978-1-4296-7705-9 (library binding)
  ISBN 978-1-4296-7924-4 (paperback)
  1. Moose—Juvenile literature. I. Title.
  QL737.U55H466 2012
  599.65'7—dc23   2011025654

Editorial Credits
Erika L. Shores, editor; Heidi Thompson, designer; Svetlana Zhurkin, media researcher;
    Kathy McColley, production specialist

Photo Credits
Corbis: Momatiuk-Eastcott, 16–17; Dreamstime: Lawrence W. Stolte, 5, Nick Gevorkyan, 18–19; iStockphoto: Doug
Lloyd, 10–11, Frank Leung, 1, 9, Ken Canning, 13; National Geographic Stock: Mattias Klum, 21; Shutterstock: Arnold
John Labrentz, cover, Chris Lorenz, 15, Steve Bower, 6–7

Note to Parents and Teachers

The North American Animals series supports national science standards related to life science.
This book describes and illustrates moose. The images support early readers in understanding
the text. The repetition of words and phrases helps early readers learn new words. This book
also introduces early readers to subject-specific vocabulary words, which are defined in the
Glossary section. Early readers may need assistance to read some words and to use the Table of
Contents, Glossary, Read More, Internet Sites, and Index sections of the book.

Printed in the United States of America in North Mankato, Minnesota.
102011   006405CGS12

Table of Contents

Living in North America

Moose travel through water and snow on long legs and tough hooves. They look for leaves to munch in northern parts of North America.

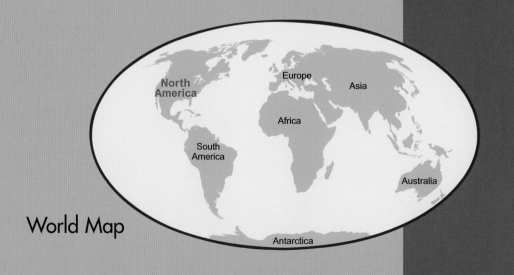

World Map

Moose live in the forests of Canada and Alaska. Moose also live in other western and northern U.S. states.

North America Map

where moose live

Up Close!

Moose are the largest members of the deer family. Male moose, called bulls, can weigh 1,600 pounds (726 kilograms). Females, called cows, weigh less.

Moose have large heads. Spoon-shaped antlers grow on a bull's head. Each year bulls shed their antlers and grow a new set.

Moose have thick fur coats.
Their coats can be light brown
to nearly black. In winter,
moose grow thicker fur
to stay warm and dry.

Eating

Moose grab leaves and twigs
with their lips and tongues.
Their front teeth clip food
into pieces. Then their back
teeth grind it.

Growing Up

Moose live alone except during mating season. Bulls and cows mate between August and October.

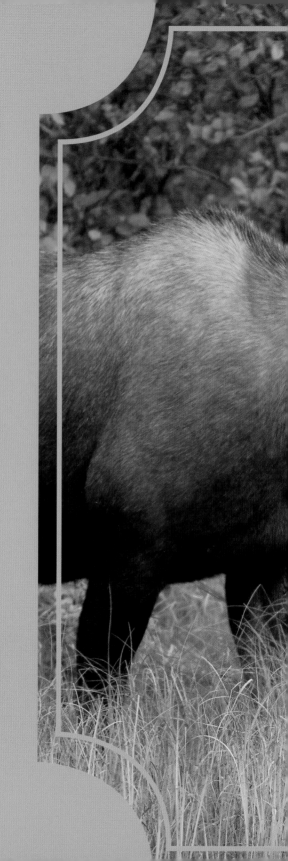

A cow gives birth to a calf between May and June. A calf drinks milk from its mother. The calf leaves its mother after about one year.

Staying Safe

Bears, wolves, and people
hunt moose. Moose stay safe
by running away.
Healthy moose live
about 16 years.

Glossary

antler—a large, branching, bony part that grows on the heads of animals in the deer family

grind—to crush or wear down

hoof—the hard covering on an animal's foot; more than one hoof is hooves

mate—to join together to produce young

shed—to drop or fall off

Read More

Arnold, Caroline. *A Moose's World.* Caroline Arnold's Animals. Minneapolis: Picture Window Books, 2010.

Gish, Melissa. *Moose.* Living Wild. Mankato, Minn.: Creative Education, 2010.

Macken, JoAnn Early. *Moose.* Animals That Live in the Forest. Pleasantville, N.Y.: Gareth Stevens Pub., 2010.

Internet Sites

FactHound offers a safe, fun way to find Internet sites related to this book. All of the sites on FactHound have been researched by our staff.

Here's all you do:

Visit *www.facthound.com*

Type in this code: 9781429677059

Super-cool stuff!

Check out projects, games and lots more at
www.capstonekids.com

Index

Word Count: 197

Grade: 1

Early-Intervention Level: 19